baring more than soul

by

remé a. grefalda

DORRANCE PUBLISHING CO., INC.
PITTSBURGH, PENNSYLVANIA 15222

All Rights Reserved
Copyright © 1997 by Remé A. Grefalda
No part of this book may be reproduced or transmitted in any form
or by any means, electronic or mechanical, including photocopying,
recording, or by any information storage and retrieval system
without permission in writing from the publisher

ISBN #0-8059-3881-8
Printed in the United States of America

First Printing

For information or to order additional books, please write:
Dorrance Publishing Co., Inc.
643 Smithfield Street
Pittsburgh, Pennsylvania 15222
U.S.A.

for Being there, thank you. . .

It starts
the way it All begins
with the ache:

seeing your unconcerned hand
and wond'ring about
your touch.

feeling the floating scent
of you surround
my whole being—

and your eyes, your eyes. . .

if they mirror my ache—
what Madness
is keeping us apart?

                        (1974)

Us two
on the head of a pin

slow-dancing
the separateness
away

savoring
the fall of liquid seconds
into endless time

look away
please

for I may never leave
your gaze

nor stop
the sense of wonder
in my heart

from gathering you

(1992)

i move
as in a mirror
to catch your fleeting eye...

willingly wait eternity
and a chasm
for that promised
Face to face.

i carry the weight
of this wrenching ache,
this longing knotted tightly
in unhinging tears—

Knowing:
Surrender at its End
will find me featherlight
in Your arms!

(1988)

for you are hesitant and shy
more halfway mine
than all.

it stands to reason
why i dream in sighs,

and close my eyes
to all your sweet response.

and dreaming, never knowing—
never knowing what is true—

how icy all the warmth we feel
compared to the Unknown!

(1964)

Now is our Moment grown:

evolving into this wakening circle,
riveting our eyes, running our feet,
inking waters
   blue with danger.

Somehow we speared our hearts, and
Singly we displaced this seething
Apathy with what they call—
   but with what we know
     as Merely
       our propensity
       for Play.

(1988)

Foolish to say
that the year begins with you.

For the year is but a mimic:
a grand copycat of every day.

Heresy to decree
that as the year begins
so shall the days follow. . .

Truth is:
my world spins madly
from that First Day—

And that day
having never reached its end

Forbids the impatient year to start!

(1962)

tomorrow is a promise

of lingering sunsets,
rose gardens and
blooms.

tomorrow
might be pain to yesterday's
bewildering joy.

tomorrow
baring her well-kept secrets
will cause confusion,
certainty, dreams...

see a garland of tomorrows
like carnival giveaways
thrown carelessly
to the world—

while you and I must pursue
a hopelessly elusive
will-o-wisp.

(1966)

I rest within the nomad callings
of my soul. I amble loose,
My bearing undefined.

Who is to say
the tunnels in our depths
are not the labyrinth to Home?

Or that our many selves
are but a prism to behold?

I'm pushed to definition
by that certain voice.
While inner longings
pause to gaze at Ambiguity:

"There is no Door. No Lock
No Single Key. To understand
is to abide in mystery.

"Suffice to know
I flow within you,
you in Me. . . ."

(1989)

Retrieve me from shadows
and Insist

    find me my life before
    I lose it

no other wildness
serves me well but yours

    so stay

or leave a trace
to resonate Those Days

for when that glorious Sun
pours out its running bleed

    I pause

before red doors
reenter shadows

only Now
in all my nakedness. . . .
I humbly gaze at You

(1993)

An orphan
by the wayside.
Her wealth were but her tears.

I had to rearrange
my world
the night I brought her in.

From then I clocked
her moments and
cued her every laugh—

But in the hands
of a beggar maid
I pawned my only
Heart!

(1961)

some yesterday tune sails in.
unwanted caller
belonging obviously to you
and yesterday.

lose you to a song?
absurd.

loving, pained, amused,
we stare:

silly, i love you
(say your eyes)
damn you, song, say I—

hold that smile!
as i whistle out of tune
some nonsense i composed,
tone-deaf in my heart.

(1968)

in boogie time
on salamander shoes
i soar

high
on some light
fantastic morn

cupping
cappucino sweets
entwined in drowsy
scents of you

who loves me
babe who loves me

i backpack queries
all day
gathering and waiting

awaiting
sunlit starlit ebony folds
unfurl a bright
and searing stillness

boogie time lost
in welcome womb
welcome full
and rushing empty

rushing madly to
welcome You

(1995)

you're afraid.
so am i.

who
would willingly stray
from spaces well-defined?

what we've stumbled on
we have easily begun.

but you insist on
Meaning,
when there is none.

i'd be content
with some
full-circled Now—

but this is all there is:

just you,
just i.

(1982)

The world abounds
with a million footsteps.

Mine are silent falterings
shadowed by your strides.

In the glare of sunlight,
through the cold blur of fog,
I see you

clearly, absurdly,
as if you were mine.

There is only you.

And you care enough to say,
"Please lock your door.
If worse comes to worst,
the Insurance Company pays."

(1963)

Not to be held,
but to be absorbed.

Not to be gazed upon,
but to be savored:
rescued like spring drops from
a petal drooped.

Not to listen,
but to sense
your musing silence
graze my virgin heart.

Not to wonder,
but to watch

the undisguised movement
of your life
within my life.
who are you, my soul's torment?

and who am I
to house
the roaring Splendor

of Your Name?

(1988)

some days
there are no hurdles:
no cloud, no pride.

some days
you sing so sinuously
through my being—

so willingly i laugh,
so willingly i learn.

(1988)

There was a time
i never dared
drink joy.

i sipped. . .

and that one slow drop
was terrifying!

Now it is single,
twin-like in me:

all that is laughter,
second nature.

Pain is sacred, looking back.
so sacred,

i hold my breath rememb'ring!

(1963)

There wasn't a foolish dream
to warn you might not care.

There was no hesitancy
in every playful wish.

This was a fancy:
a lighthearted spring of the heart

Requiring no pain
to make it last,

Nor throbbing fear,
permitting Certainty.

This was a drop of lonely sweetness
rescued from discarded dreams—

But you brought in heartache anyway.

(1966)

I died a little
as I read
the Notice
in my hands.

It told me all I longed
to know—
one Doubt was left
to stand.

But Life
could not combat
nor stop the truth
now strangling me.

One kiss
upon the hand that signed,
I faced Eternity.

(1961)

did i come this far
only to walk away?

why now is the space elusive
and the once-upon gone

when they created us:

the two of us, like twins
separate from the world?

have i reached this far—

only to tread in sheer want?
be left aching and
bewildered

by your constant No.

(1983)

and if i cried
the tears would mock
my foolish hoard of pains.

illegitimate i stand:
a bastard child
shunned with proper courtesy.

O Fancies,
my wishful, never-ending dreams!
O must you call me now

to seek
my customary refuge
within your Mammy-heart?

(1962)

I have not lost you with a tear.

A drop for Grief
would be too precious now
to fall.

Shall I lament
and full expose
my wretched self?

Then you would rule me
—would you not?—
in ruth, if not in scorn.

I have not perked pretense
nor jest in artful gaiety.

The Masks
the world has worn
would never fit on me.

                    (1962)

The wrong you sowed
upon my barren fields
is rooted deep and
shades my lonely world,

The sin is ours:

Am I not solely thine?
But grieving thus
the suffering soul is mine.

Perhaps I should have plucked
the Roots
before the tree
had grown. . .

One last alternative remains:

But, can I cut it down?

(1962)

you never left me.

i made myself believe
you would stay for the span
a lifetime would allow.

once i was soft, yielding,
and brazenly warm
to your probing lips.

i would dare all hostile looks
upon my coat of many colors
shrugging off envy with a laugh.

you were there, then. . .

smiling amused, silently proud
of the wild soaring youth
in my heart.

but they were never hostile—
they were the kind, all-knowing

eyes of the world
warning me to curb my flight
lest i rise in splinters
after the fall.

yes, after the free fall

. . .i no longer shiver
at a gust of wind.
for as cold as wind,
i am cold.

bereft of you
i exist—
echoing laughter
as brittle as forgotten twigs.

(1966)

Emptied of my hoardings,
I counted out
my dreams.

Some seemed
unable to survive,
a few were petty schemes.

I chanced on One
just fading. . .
lifted it, tippy-toe
High—

I felt a wink
more powerful than
a Wand,

and Knew
I'd take my time
just wait!

                    (1988)

She asked
if I was certain.
Reluctance
told me I was sure:

"If you stop to think now
—Uncertainty
will rule."

So took my Heart,
with one last look
I hurled it
to the Sea. . .

Once in every Century,
the world needs
a Fool.

(1961)

Apart we stand alone:

our hearts
in mad pursuit
for each a world to own.

In this estrangement
somehow
we will meet

soul to soul
in seconds snatched
from timeless space.

for still in you
the Waif
cries tearless
for the Strong in me.

and Child once tendered
by those Gentle Hands
is still a Me in me.

(1961)

A holiday affair
    festooned and
        brightened by
    a gathered glow
    from ember-hearts
Unbridled play
    intensified
        heightened by cliffs
        and brushings 'gainst
        razorblade walls
When fearful Brave
    and trembling Soul meet
      but wonder
        whether to touch at all
Wonder if you will
    but Claim what is Yours
        what has Been There
           and Written So
    For we are here
Capsuled in this holy moment
    and we were There
When all of Time began

                (1993)

when you said
get up and walk
we couldn't

awed as we all were

(why was it so hard
to take that
first step)

it took your touch

the warmth to lift
the hold to pull
my stubborn foot
out of the clutch

awed as i was (and still am)
i never thanked you

I simply walked away

(1994)

Enough
that you trust me
with the Mystery.

Invite me to Stillness
and firefly waltzes
and insights of rainbow

All in the Dark.

Enough too,
that I remain
Sentinel to dreams,

collecting oceans
in between,
even if you never cross
the drying sands.

Still
You insist on More,
when I am loved
and gift-content.

For if I havent found
the vessel to contain
Enough—

how more
a basket for the overflow?

(1990)

Singed by your mere thought.

When split into words
and heard
by voice alone
Loved

By you
reaching out.
When you rustle still air
by mere voice

You touch me,
stirring waters of my soul.

Play me
Set me once more
Sum apart

To yearn to seek
if merely to see
through a prism

. . .

In quiet loving
All while merely
Loving You.

(1992)